Sports on the Edge

Brian Sargent

Contents

Rigby

A Harcourt Achieve Imprint

www.Rigby.com
1-800-531-5015

The crowd watches as the skateboarder skates to the top of the ramp. He flies into the air and spins around with his skateboard. He skates back down the ramp and up the other side. At the top of the other side, he does a handstand on one hand. The crowd yells and cheers, and the judges say he has won the contest!

skateboarding

Skateboarding is one type of extreme sport. Other extreme sports are snowboarding, inline skating, and surfing. These sports are called *extreme* because they often combine danger, speed, height, and difficult tricks. The people who do extreme sports often push themselves to go faster, jump higher, or do harder tricks.

Each of these extreme sports is different, and each one has its own history. But all of these sports started because somebody tried something new and exciting.

inline skating

snowboarding

surfing

Chapter 2

Skateboarding

The Skateboard Then and Now

The first skateboards were very different from the ones we see today. They were wooden boxes with clay wheels, and they were noisy and hard to steer. Then in the 1970s, a skateboarder named Frank Nasworthy had an idea. He decided to replace the clay wheels with plastic wheels. The new wheels were smoother than the old wheels and made the skateboards easier to control. After that skateboarding became much more popular.

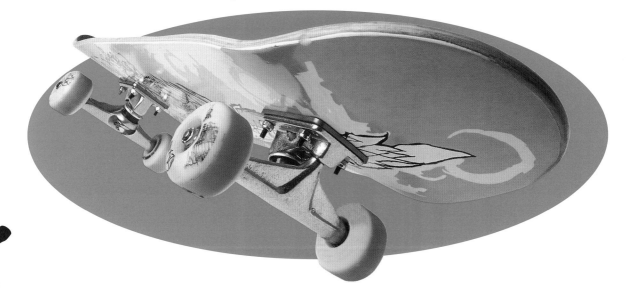

Types of Skateboarding

Two types of skateboarding are freestyle and vertical. In freestyle skateboarding, skateboarders do tricks on a flat surface. The word *vertical* means "straight up and down," so in vertical skateboarding, skateboarders perform tricks by going up and down a ramp. A ramp is a surface with a slope.

One trick is called a *360*. In a 360, the skateboarder skates to the top of the ramp and turns around once in the air.

This skateboarder is doing a trick on a ramp.

5

Tony Hawk

One of the most famous skateboarders is Tony Hawk. By the time he was 16 years old, he was the best skateboarder in the world. In 1999 he was the first person to do a trick called the *900*. In this trick, he skated to the top of the ramp and spun around several times in the air. In 2002 he started a group called the Tony Hawk Foundation. This group helps communities build skateparks where kids can skate.

Skateboard Explosion!

That same year, Tony Hawk's popularity exploded with the launch of Boom-Boom HuckJam.

Boom-Boom HuckJam is an action-packed city tour that features the best skaters in the world of skateboarding. Athletes from across the globe dream about participating in this exciting competition and the chance to skate alongside the legendary Tony Hawk!

Flying High!

Skateboarding continues to expand to all parts of the planet. One organization that's increasing the sport's popularity is called *Skate Australia.* The organization is the first of its kind to create a national program designed to teach young skateboarders and improve their abilities.

Figure It Out

Let's figure out how many turns are in a 900 trick. The **data,** or information, in the **table** below shows some different skateboarding tricks.

Name of Trick	Number of Turns in the Air
180	1/2 turn
360	1 turn
540	1 1/2 turns
720	2 turns
900	?

Look for a pattern in the number of turns. A **pattern** is a number that repeats. If the pattern continues, how many turns will there be in a 900 trick?

Answer: 2 1/2 turns

Chapter 3

Snowboarding

The First Snowboard

In 1965 a man watched his 11-year-old daughter ride down a snowy hill, standing on a sled! This gave him a great idea. He rushed inside his house, tied two skis together, and attached a string to the tip for steering. He called it a Snurfer, and one year later, he sold his idea to a company. The company soon began to make Snurfers and sold them for about $20.00 each.

Snurfers were the first snowboards. They were very popular, but many people didn't think that they would stay popular. Truly, those people must be surprised to know that snowboarding is now an Olympic sport!

Many people consider the Snurfer to be the first snowboard.

Skiing and Snowboarding

Skiing and snowboarding are both winter sports that require snow. But there are also differences between the two sports. In skiing, the skier uses two boards, but in snowboarding, the snowboarder uses only one board. Skiers also use poles, but snowboarders don't.

Snowboarding at the Olympic Games

In 1998 snowboarding became the first extreme sport to be in the Olympic Games. In the games, snowboarders could enter two possible events, the slalom and the halfpipe. In the slalom, snowboarders race down a slope, moving between poles with flags on them. In the halfpipe, snowboarders do tricks on a course shaped like a giant U.

Family Ties

At the 2006 Olympic Games, Philipp and Simon Schoch took home the gold and silver medals for slalom snowboarding. The two brothers have been snowboarding together since they were kids and raced against each other during the winter games.

At the end of the race, Philipp became the first person ever to win two Olympic gold medals for slalom snowboarding. Simon came in second, winning the silver medal.

At the Top of Their Game

Women's snowboarding is gaining a lot of support. Millions of fans screamed with excitement during the 2006 Winter Olympics as Hannah Teter and Gretchen Bleiler claimed the gold and silver medals following the halfpipe competition.

Figure It Out

Daniel is a snowboarder, and he has been practicing for the Olympics. The table below shows how long it took Daniel to snowboard down the slope for each attempt.

Attempt	Time
1	2 minutes 30 seconds
2	2 minutes 22 seconds
3	2 minutes 14 seconds
4	?

Look at Daniel's time for each attempt. If the pattern continues, what will be his time for his fourth attempt?

Answer: 2 minutes 6 seconds

Inline skating is an older sport than both skateboarding and snowboarding. The first inline skates were made in 1819, and each skate had only three wheels. The wheels were large and made of metal, and it was very difficult for the skater to turn. Modern inline skates have four plastic wheels in one line and are easier to control.

the first inline skate

modern inline skates

Skating Tricks

Like skateboarders, inline skaters also do tricks on a ramp. Many of the tricks send the skater high into the air.

One inline skating trick is called a *360*. When skaters do a 360, they spin completely around, as if they are skating in a circle. Inline skaters need special gear to keep them safe. This gear protects them when they are doing tricks such as the 360.

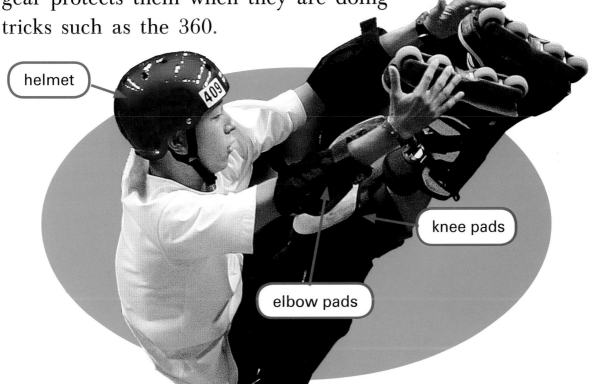

helmet

knee pads

elbow pads

Oh, Brother!

The Yasutoko brothers are two of the most famous inline skaters in the world. At the 2004 Asian X Games, 17-year-old Takeshi Yasutoko won the gold medal with a score of 98.25. This is the highest score ever recorded at the Asian X Games! His brother Eito is equally impressive. Eito's ability to spin 1440 degrees— 4 full rotations—amazes fans all over the world!

Figure It Out

In New Town, inline skating is becoming very popular. The table below shows the number of inline skaters at the park at the end of each week.

Week	Number of Skaters
1	10
2	12
3	15
4	17
5	20
6	?

Look for a pattern in the number of skaters. If the pattern continues, how many skaters will be at the park at the end of the sixth week?

Answer: 22

The Original Extreme Sport

The original extreme sport is surfing. Surfing started on the islands of Hawaii and has a very long history. People don't really know exactly when the sport began, but some people believe that surfing may have started as many as 1,600 years ago.

Long ago, the Hawaiian people called surfing *wave sliding.* Surfing was a very important sport for the chiefs of Hawaii who often showed their skill by surfing big waves.

The Father of Modern Surfing

The man people call the Father of Modern Surfing was named Duke Kahanamoku, but most people just called him Duke. Duke was born in 1890 in Hawaii. He was an excellent swimmer and surfer, so he would often travel to different countries and teach people about surfing. Duke put on many surfing shows in the United States and around the world. People would crowd the beach just to watch him surf.

Duke was called "The Human Fish" because he was a fast swimmer.

Surfing and Waves

Good surfing needs good waves, and good waves need good wind. The best places to surf in the United States are in Hawaii and on the West Coast. On the West Coast, the wind usually travels with the waves, making them stronger.

Surfing Basics

Check the water level.

↓

Put on a ski vest.

↓

Put the surfboard leash around your ankle.

↓

Paddle out in the water until you see the tops of the waves.

↓

Surf between the top and the base of the wave.

Wave Speed and Wave Height

In the diagram, you can see how wind speed, measured in miles per hour, changes the height of a wave. When the wind gets stronger, the waves get bigger. A 35-mile-per-hour wind can create a wave that is 18 feet high, or three times as tall as a person!

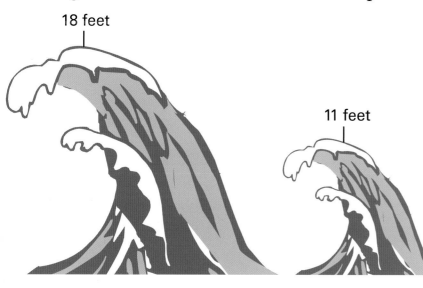

18 feet

11 feet

8 feet

3 feet

35 miles per hour

29 miles per hour

23 miles per hour

17 miles per hour

Kelly Slater is one of the most famous professional surfers today. He is originally from Cocoa Beach, California, and has won a total of seven world championships. His amazing talent and countless victories are the reasons many people call Kelly the greatest surfer of all time.

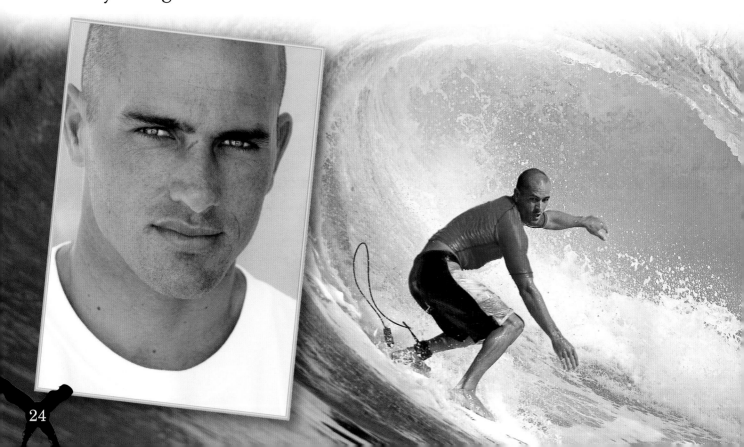

Figure It Out

Surfers practice for hours and hours in the water. They also pay very close attention to the water level. The table below shows the depth of the water at different times of the day near a popular beach.

Time of Day	Water Depth
6:00 A.M.	6 ft
8:00 A.M.	9 ft
10:00 A.M.	12 ft
12:00 P.M.	?

Look for a pattern in the depth of the water. If the pattern continues, what will the water level be at 12:00 P.M.?

Answer: 15 ft

Chapter 6

The X Games and Beyond

In 1993 a sports television network had an idea. It decided to create a contest for extreme sports called the Extreme Games. The first Extreme Games were in 1995, and there were 27 different events. (After the first year, the network changed the name to the X Games.) Since 1997 there have been both summer and winter X Games, and the games have become more popular each year. People come from all over the world to compete in the X Games.

In 1999 inline skaters from 12 different countries skated in the X Games.

That Girl Can Skate!

One event at the X Games is the Women's Inline Skating Vertical event. In this event, skaters do tricks on a halfpipe ramp. One of the best inline skaters in the world is Fabiola da Silva from Brazil. She started skating when she was eight years old, and since 1996, she has won five gold medals and one silver medal in the vertical event at the X Games. In fact, she is so good that she skates in the men's event, too. In the men's event, the skaters jump higher and do more difficult tricks.

Fabiola waves to the crowd.

27

With so many wins, it's no wonder people think of Fabiola as one of the best inline skaters of all time. She continues to impress fans at the X Games and in other contests throughout the world.

What's Next for Extreme Sports?

The people who do extreme sports often try things that can be dangerous. An inline skater might do a 360. A surfer might surf a wave that is two or three times his height. A skateboarder might fly very high into the air, and a snowboarder might do a trick on a halfpipe. Because these people push themselves to do things that are new and difficult, extreme sports will continue to change. Who knows what extreme sport they will think of next?

1819
The first inline
skate is made.

1937
Surfboards are made and sold
by a company for the first time.

1972
Skateboards are made
with plastic wheels.

1820	1840	1860	1880	1900

1890
Duke, the Father of
Modern Surfing, is born.

1965
The Snurfer is invented.

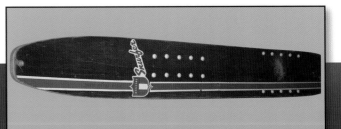

Time Line of Extreme Sports

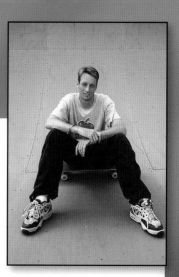

1995
The Extreme Games, or X Games, begin.

1999
Tony Hawk is the first person to do a 900.

| 1920 | 1940 | 1960 | 1980 | 2000 |

1980
The first modern inline skates are made.

1998
Snowboarding becomes an Olympic sport.

Glossary

data information
table a way to show data in rows and columns
pattern numbers that repeat in a certain order

Index